Wordly Wise
BOOK C

Kenneth Hodkinson

EDUCATORS PUBLISHING SERVICE
Cambridge and Toronto

Introduction to *Wordly Wise A, B,* and *C*

The *Wordly Wise ABC* series of vocabulary books helps students to think not only about words and how we define them but also about the world of things and ideas for which words are referents.

A student may "know" what an elephant is, but how would she or he define *elephant*? Book A offers a definition of the word that is sufficiently broad to encompass both the Indian and African varieties; it follows this with an illustrative sentence that explains the ways in which the two types differ; it also includes a drawing that shows these differences.

Eight to twelve words are covered in each lesson in similar fashion. Some of these words the student will "know"; some he or she will not know. For some words, one meaning may be known but not other, less common, meanings.

Every vocabulary word in Book A has an accompanying picture (a nonverbal definition). The frequency of pictures in relation to the text is reduced from Book A to B and from B to C.

All three books in the *ABC* series test and reinforce the student's understanding of the meanings of the words on the Word List in a True/False exercise. Here the student is required to discriminate between a correct (True) and an incorrect (False) definition for each meaning of each word.

After this comes a Hidden Message puzzle that challenges the student to find the answer to a riddle by matching definitions with words from the Word List.

Then comes a Crossword Puzzle; the clues are illustrative sentences (different from those on the Word List pages) with one word, taken from the Word List, missing. This word, if correctly chosen, fits the puzzle. Book A has an additional feature, a set of pictorial clues incorporated into the crossword diagram.

Book C has an additional exercise in which the student replaces a cumbersome phrase with a single word from the Word List. This prepares the student for Book 1 of the *Wordly Wise* Books 1–9 series. The definitions and illustrative sentences are confined to a single page of dictionary format to accommodate this additional exercise, and the crossword puzzles in Book C appear as review exercises after two lessons. (In Book 1, crossword puzzles appear after every three lessons.)

Illustrator: Dana Franzen

© 1998, 1990, 1981 by Educators Publishing Service, a division of School Specialty Publishing, a member of the School Specialty Family. All rights reserved. No part of this book may be reproduced or utilized in any form or by any electronic or mechanical means, including photocopying, without permission in writing from the publisher.

Printed in USA

ISBN 978-0-8388-0430-8

18 19 20 PPG 17 16

WORD LIST

adopt (6)*
adult (11)
album (11)
appetite (5)
artery (2)
athlete (12)
author (11)
autograph (12)

bait (8)
balcony (12)
barge (9)
barometer (5)
bead (11)
beeline (10)
brand (12)
burglar (1)

canal (11)
clang (10)
clutter (1)
code (5)
comb (11)
constable (2)
crow (5)
cube (3)
cue (7)
cymbal (7)

dairy (6)
denim (4)
dent (5)
detour (6)
diamond (9)
disappear (12)
discard (6)
drowsy (6)
duet (1)

eavesdrop (10)
elastic (1)
ember (9)
evacuate (10)
evil (12)

fleece (9)
florist (4)
foe (10)
frustrate (4)
furrow (1)

grain (6)
granite (5)
gray (9)

habit (4)
hutch (8)

island (3)

junk (4)

kiosk (3)

ladle (2)
late (3)
lecture (11)
local (4)
locket (9)
luxury (8)

magic (8)
margin (8)
mascot (8)
mental (5)
moat (10)
murmur (7)

ornament (7)
oval (3)
owe (6)

pang (6)
perish (7)
portrait (9)
prod (8)
profile (10)

recipe (1)
reptile (3)
ripe (2)
rodeo (4)

sculptor (4)
sheaf (3)
sift (10)
steam (10)
stirrup (2)
straddle (8)
suburb (11)
surf (9)

tablet (1)
target (2)
tenant (4)
tomahawk (9)
tongs (12)
traitor (6)
trellis (2)
tutor (9)

unicorn (7)

violet (11)
vivid (12)
volcano (3)

warehouse (3)
wedge (10)
whittle (7)
widow (1)
widower (2)
wisp (5)

yard (7)

zero (3)

*Numbers in parentheses refer to the Word List in which the word appears.

WORD LIST 1

burglar   elastic   tablet
clutter   furrow   widow
duet   recipe

burglar—(noun) a person who breaks into a building, especially at night, in order to steal: *A burglar broke into the house next door and stole a gold ring.*

clutter—(noun) a mess of things piled together or scattered about: *Somewhere among the clutter in the basement are my skates.* —(verb) to fill with useless things or ideas in no sort of order: *Don't clutter your closet with clothes you never wear. Don't clutter your mind with silly TV shows.*

duet—(noun) **1.** a piece of music for two singers or two musical instruments: *The program ended with a duet for violin and piano.* **2.** two people who play music or sing together: *Maria and Carlos have formed a duet and will be singing at the concert tonight.*

elastic—(noun) cloth tape with rubber threads in it to make it stretch: *Elastic is sewn into the waist of pajama pants so that they will stay up.*—(adjective) able to spring back to the same shape or size after being stretched or squeezed: *This elastic belt will stretch to fit your waist.*

furrow—(noun) a long, narrow groove or cut made by a plow turning over the earth: *A good farmer plows a straight furrow.*—(verb) to make a groove or wrinkle in: *I saw him furrow his brow as he thought about the question.*

recipe—(noun) **1.** a list of things needed and things to do to make something to eat or drink: *This recipe for pancakes calls for two eggs.* **2.** a way to have or to get something: *She said her recipe for a long life was to work hard, eat well, and get enough rest.*

tablet—(noun) **1.** a small, flattish pill: *She bought a bottle of vitamin C tablets at the health-food store.* **2.** sheets of writing paper made into a pad: *I bought a writing tablet and some envelopes at the store.* **3.** a thin, flat block of metal or stone with writing on it. *A metal tablet set into the rock at Plymouth says the Pilgrims landed at that spot.*

widow—(noun) a woman whose husband has died and who has not married again: *The widow has three small children to raise by herself.*

EXERCISE 1A

Some of the sentences below are true and some are false. On the line to the left of each sentence, write _T_ if you think the sentence is true, and _F_ if you think the sentence is false.

_____ 1. A burglar is a woman whose husband has died.

_____ 2. A burglar is a person who breaks into a building to steal.

_____ 3. Clutter is a mess of things piled together or scattered about.

_____ 4. To clutter is to fill with useless things or ideas in no sort of order.

_____ 5. A duet is a piece of music for two singers or two musical instruments.

_____ 6. A duet is two people who play music or sing together.

_____ 7. Elastic means able to spring back to the same size after being stretched or squeezed.

_____ 8. Elastic is sheets of writing paper made into a pad.

_____ 9. A furrow is a long, narrow groove or cut made by a plow turning over the earth.

_____ 10. To furrow is to make a groove or wrinkle in something.

_____ 11. A recipe is a list of things needed and things to do to make something to eat or drink.

_____ 12. A recipe is a way to have or to get something.

_____ 13. A tablet is a thin, flat block of metal or stone with writing on it.

_____ 14. A tablet is a small, flattish pill.

_____ 15. A widow is a child whose parents have died.

_____ 16. A widow is a woman whose husband has died and who has not married again.

Check your answers against the correct ones below. They are not in order. This is to prevent your eye from catching sight of the correct answers before you have had a chance to do the exercise on your own.

| 10 T. | 4 T. | 16 T. | 7 T. | 13 T. | 2 T. | 9 T. | 11 T. |
| 5 T. | 1 F. | 14 T. | 3 T. | 12 T. | 6 T. | 15 F. | 8 F. |

EXERCISE 1B

Rewrite each sentence below. Replace the underlined words with the correct vocabulary word from Word List 1.

1. Next Saturday we will clean up the <u>mess of things all piled together</u> in the empty lot on the corner.

   _____

   _____

2. The <u>woman whose husband had died</u> wept as she knelt at the graveside.

   _____

3. A <u>flat metal block with writing on it</u> on the wall said that the school was named after Elizabeth Fry, the Quaker who spent her life helping people in prison.

   _____

   _____

4. If you are going to make hot chili, you will need to look up the <u>list of things needed and things to do</u>.

   _____

   _____

5. The <u>person who broke into the house in order to steal</u> got away with coins worth thousands of dollars.

   _____

   _____

6. The <u>long, narrow groove made by the plow turning over the earth</u> can be made deeper by lowering the blade on the plow.

   _____

   _____

7. They sang the <u>love song for two voices</u> from the opera *Carmen*.

   _____

   _____

8. You can use this piece of <u>cloth with rubber threads running through it</u> to make a sling shot.

   _____

   _____

EXERCISE 1C

In the boxes next to each definition, write the correct vocabulary word from Word List 1.
Put one letter in each box. If you do this properly, the long boxes running from top to bottom
will answer the following riddle:

What's the difference between an old penny and a new nickel?

1. able to spring back to the same shape or size after being
   stretched or squeezed

2. a small, flattish pill

3. two people who play music or sing together

4. a mess of things piled together or scattered about

5. to make a groove or wrinkle in

6. a woman whose husband has died and who has not
   married again

7. to fill with useless things or ideas in no sort of order

8. a person who breaks into a building, especially at night, in
   order to steal

9. a way to have or to get something

10. a list of things needed and things to do to make something to
    eat or drink

11. sheets of writing paper made into a pad

12. cloth tape with rubber threads in it to make it stretch

WORD LIST 2

artery   ripe   trellis
constable   stirrup   widower
ladle   target

artery—(noun) a tube or blood vessel that carries blood from the heart to all parts of the body: *The main artery from the heart branches into many smaller blood vessels.*

constable—(noun) a British police office of the lowest rank: *I was not used to driving in Britain and was soon stopped by a constable.*

ladle—(noun) a cuplike spoon with a long handle, used for serving anything liquid: *Dip the ladle in the bowl of fruit punch and fill the glass from it.*—(verb) to serve anything that can be scooped up with a ladle or cuplike spoon: *Ladle everyone a bowl of stew.*

ripe—(adjective) **1.** ready to be picked and eaten: *Martin got a stomach ache from eating apples that weren't ripe.* **2.** ready for some action or purpose: *The time is now ripe for us to act.*

stirrup—(noun) either of the two metal rings with flat bottoms that hang from straps fastened to each side of a horse's saddle: *Keep each foot firmly in a stirrup so that you can control the horse properly.*

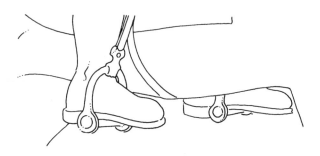

target—(noun) **1.** something that is aimed at and shot at: *The middle ring of the target is called the bull's-eye.* **2.** a person or thing that is attacked or made fun of: *He was the target of all their teasing.* **3.** a goal or objective: *My target this year is to get all A's in school.*

trellis—(noun) a crisscross of thin wooden strips made into a frame on which plants can climb: *The end of the garden is screened off with a trellis covered with climbing roses.*

widower—(noun) a man whose wife has died and who has not married again: *Mr. Shen's wife died when he was very young, and he remained a widower all his life.*

EXERCISE 2A

Some of the sentences below are true and some are false. On the line to the left of each sentence, write *T* if you think the sentence is true, and *F* if you think the sentence is false.

_____ 1. An artery is a tube or blood vessel that carries blood from the heart.

_____ 2. An artery is a tube or blood vessel that carries blood to the heart.

_____ 3. A constable is a metal ring with a flat bottom that hangs from a strap fastened to the side of a horse's saddle.

_____ 4. A constable is a British police officer of the lowest rank.

_____ 5. To ladle is to serve anything that can be scooped up with a long-handled, cuplike spoon.

_____ 6. A ladle is a cuplike spoon with a long handle used for serving anything liquid.

_____ 7. Ripe means ready to be picked and eaten.

_____ 8. Ripe means ready for some action or purpose.

_____ 9. A stirrup is either of the two metal rings with flat bottoms that hang from straps fastened to each side of a horse's saddle.

_____ 10. A stirrup is a crisscross of thin wooden strips made into a frame on which plants can climb.

_____ 11. A target is something that is aimed at and shot at.

_____ 12. A target is a person or thing that is attacked or made fun of.

_____ 13. A trellis is a mess of things piled together in no sort of order.

_____ 14. A trellis is a crisscross of thin wooden strips made into a frame on which plants can climb.

_____ 15. A widower is a man whose wife has died and who has not married again.

_____ 16. A widower is a woman whose husband has died and who has not married again.

Check your answers against the correct ones below. They are not in order. This is to prevent your eye from catching sight of the correct answers before you have had a chance to do the exercise on your own.

6 T.	11 T.	2 F.	16 F.	9 T.	5 T.	15 T.	1 T.
13 F.	4 T.	10 F.	7 T.	3 F.	14 T.	8 T.	12 T.

EXERCISE 2B

Rewrite each sentence below. Replace the underlined words with the correct vocabulary word from Word List 2.

1. The largest <u>tube that carries blood from the heart to other parts of the body</u> is called the aorta.

_____

_____

2. The rider's foot had come out of the <u>metal ring with a flat bottom that hangs from the saddle.</u>

_____

_____

3. Use this <u>cuplike spoon with a long handle</u> to serve the soup.

_____

_____

4. You can buy the <u>frame of crisscross strips of wood</u> in six-foot sections that you fasten together.

_____

_____

5. The <u>police officer of the lowest rank in England</u> was very helpful when we got lost.

_____

_____

6. I think these cherries are <u>ready to be picked and eaten.</u>

_____

_____

7. The old <u>man whose wife had died</u> often told us how much he missed his wife.

_____

_____

8. The <u>object used to aim at and shoot at</u> was a tin can set on top of a wall.

_____

_____

EXERCISE 2C

**In the boxes next to each definition, write the correct vocabulary word from Word List 2.
Put one letter in each box. If you do this properly, the long boxes running from top to bottom
will answer the following riddle:**

Who can talk to Silver but not to Gold?

1. a tube or blood vessel that carries blood from the heart to all parts of the body

2. ready to be picked and eaten

3. a cuplike spoon with a long handle, used for serving anything liquid

4. a man whose wife has died and who has not married again

5. a British police officer of the lowest rank

6. ready for some action or purpose

7. a crisscross of thin wooden strips made into a frame on which plants can climb

8. something that is aimed at and shot at

9. a person or thing made fun of or attacked

10. to serve by scooping up with a long-handled spoon

11. either of two metal rings with flat bottoms that hang from straps attached to both sides of a saddle

9

CROSSWORD 1

Decide what word from Word List 1 or 2 is missing from each sentence below. For the first group of sentences (Clues Across), write each answer in the boxes running across on the puzzle on the next page. For the second group (Clues Down), write each answer in the boxes running down.

Work out the sentences in any order you like; just be sure to match the number of the sentence with the number in the box. Put only one letter in each box. If all your answers are correct, all the words on the puzzle will fit together.

Clues Across

5. The police say they have caught the _____ who broke into the bank two nights ago.

7. He took an aspirin _____, hoping that his headache would go away.

9. The grave of the woman was marked by a stone _____ giving her name and the dates of her birth and death.

10. She refused to get angry when they called her names, so they looked for another _____ for their cruel jokes.

12. I asked him for the _____ for his "camper's stew."

13. You serve the rice, and I will _____ out the beans from the pot.

14. The two girls played the _____ beautifully.

17. The little boy searched through the _____ of toys to find his favorite stuffed animal.

20. Use the _____ to serve the chowder because it's quicker than using a spoon.

21. His _____ for success is hard work, more hard work, and still more hard work.

22. After a few years, the young _____ remarried.

25. If you need help while in Britain, just look around for the nearest _____.

Clues Down

1. Ms. Wong tore off a sheet from the _____ on her desk and wrote down my phone number.

2. The _____ that supports the vines is quite old and needs to be strengthened before it falls over.

3. The _____ of hamburger stands, pizza parlors, and used car lots along the highway bothers many people.

4. If an _____ is blocked, the blood cannot flow properly.

6. To get on the horse, put your hands on the saddle, place a foot in one _____, and swing yourself up.

8. Sally's _____ was to read fifteen books this summer.

11. This rubber band is very _____ and will expand to three times its length.

15. I saw the plane _____ the ground when it landed in the field with its wheels jammed in the up position.

16. We tried to comfort the _____ after the death of her husband.

18. The corn turns golden when it is _____.

19. Don't stretch the _____ when you measure off the length you need.

23. Two of the singers left the group and formed a _____.

24. I could see the children were _____ for mischief, so I told them to settle down.

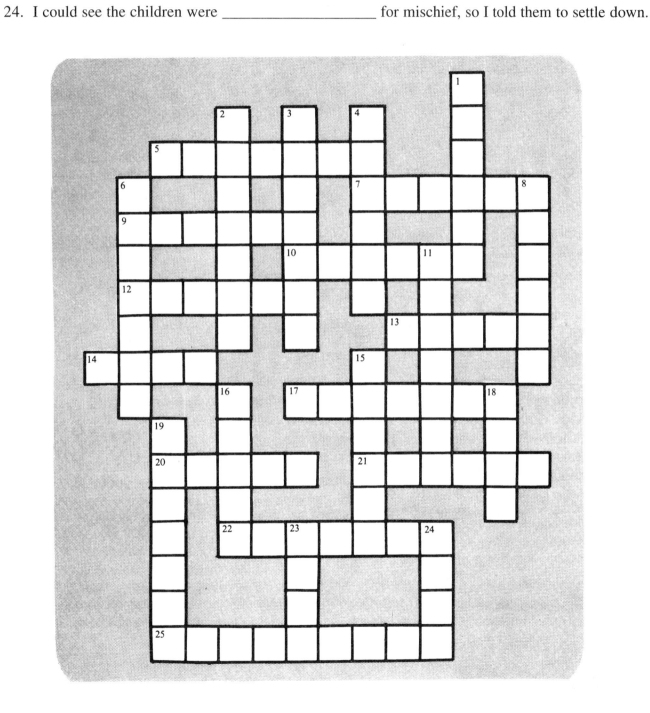

WORD LIST 3

cube	late	volcano
island	oval	warehouse
kiosk	reptile	zero
	sheaf	

cube—(noun) a solid shape with six square sides: *Dice are cubes marked on each side with from one to six dots.*—(verb) to cut up into cubes: *Cube the melon and put it in the fruit salad.*

island—(noun) a piece of land that is surrounded by water: *Australia is an extremely large island.*

kiosk—(noun) a small open building where items like magazines and candy are sold: *I buy my newspaper from the kiosk outside the train station.*

late—(adjective) **1.** happening or coming after the expected time: *The seven o'clock train will be ten minutes late.* **2.** having been dead just a short time: *I knew the late Mr. Swenson very well, and I was sorry to hear that he had died.*—(adverb) coming at or near the end: *Christmas comes late in the year.*

oval—(noun) a shape like a stretched-out circle: *This is an oval ◯, and so is this 0.* —(adjective) having the shape of a stretched-out circle: *She has an oval face.*

reptile—(noun) any of a large number of cold-blooded animals with a backbone and scaly or hard, rough skin: *A crocodile is a reptile, and so was a brontosaurus.*

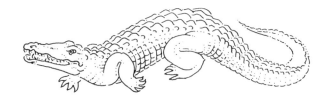

sheaf—(noun) **1.** a lot of long stalks of wheat, oats, or other cereal plant, cut and tied in a bundle: *Take this wheat sheaf and stack it with the others.* **2.** a pile or bundle of things of the same kind: *She let the bills stack up on her desk until there was quite a sheaf of them.*

volcano—(noun) a mountain with a hole in the top from which ash, steam, and hot melted rock may be thrown: *Parts of Oregon and Washington were covered with ash when the volcano known as Mount St. Helens became active.*

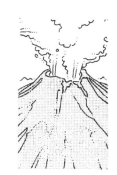

warehouse—(noun) a large building used for storing things before they are sold: *Things made in a factory go to a warehouse before they are sent out to stores.*

zero—(noun) **1.** the number that stands for nothing, written *0: Four minus four equals zero.* **2.** the temperature from which all other temperatures are measured, usually that at which water freezes: *It dropped to fifteen degrees below zero last night, the coldest night of the winter so far.*

EXERCISE 3A

Some of the sentences below are true and some are false. On the line to the left of each sentence, write *T* if you think the sentence is true, and *F* if you think the sentence is false.

_____ 1. A cube is a solid shape with six square sides.

_____ 2. To cube is to cut up into dice-shaped pieces.

_____ 3. An island is a piece of land surrounded by water.

_____ 4. An island is a stretch of water surrounded by land.

_____ 5. A kiosk is a shape like a stretched-out circle.

_____ 6. A kiosk is a small open building where magazines, candy, and other such items are sold.

_____ 7. Late means happening or coming after the expected time.

_____ 8. Late means coming at or near the end.

_____ 9. An oval is a shape like a stretched-out circle.

_____ 10. An oval is a solid shape with six square sides.

_____ 11. A reptile is a cold-blooded animal with a backbone and scaly or hard, rough skin.

_____ 12. A reptile is a person who breaks into a house to steal.

_____ 13. A sheaf is a pile or bundle of things of the same kind.

_____ 14. A sheaf is a bundle of stalks of a cereal plant.

_____ 15. A volcano is a strong wind that whirls around in a circle.

_____ 16. A volcano is a mountain with a hole in the top from which steam, ash, and hot melted rock may be thrown.

_____ 17. A warehouse is a small open building where magazines, candy, and other such items are sold.

_____ 18. A warehouse is a large building used for storing things before they are sold.

_____ 19. Zero is the number that stands for nothing.

_____ 20. Zero is the temperature from which all other temperatures are measured.

Check your answers against the correct ones below. They are not in order. This is to prevent your eye from catching sight of the correct answers before you have had a chance to do the exercise on your own.

12 F.	16 T.	2 T.	5 F.	20 T.	11 T.	6 T.	17 F.	10 F.	18 T.
13 T.	4 F.	1 T.	14 T.	8 T.	3 T.	15 F.	9 T.	19 T.	7 T.

EXERCISE 3B

Rewrite each sentence below. Replace the underlined words with the correct vocabulary word from Word List 3.

1. An alligator is a <u>cold-blooded animal with a scaly skin.</u>

   _____

   _____

2. It is ten degrees above <u>the temperature from which all other temperatures are measured.</u>

   _____

   _____

3. Ask the woman who runs the <u>small open building where candy and magazines are sold</u> to change this dollar bill.

   _____

   _____

4. The <u>recently dead</u> Mrs. Gomez was a good friend of mine.

   _____

   _____

5. Our kitchen table is square, but our neighbor's is <u>shaped like a stretched-out circle.</u>

   _____

   _____

6. A <u>solid shape with six square sides</u> has eight corners.

   _____

   _____

7. Each <u>tied up bundle of long stalks</u> of corn is left outside to dry in the sun.

   _____

   _____

8. During the tour of the candy factory, the class got to see the <u>large building where things are stored</u>, which was filled with large boxes of candy.

   _____

   _____

EXERCISE 3C

In the boxes next to each definition, write the correct vocabulary word from Word List 3.
Put one letter in each box. If you do this properly, the long boxes running from top to bottom
will answer the following riddle:

When Silly Billy's girlfriend asked for a pair of slippers, what did Silly Billy give her?

1. having been dead just a short time

2. the number that stands for nothing, written *0*

3. to cut up into dice-shaped pieces

4. coming at or near the end

5. a piece of land surrounded by water

6. a pile or bundle of things of the same kind

7. a mountain with a hole in the top from which ash,
   steam, and hot melted rock may be thrown

8. happening or coming after the expected time

9. a cold-blooded animal with a backbone and scaly or hard,
   rough skin

10. a large building where things are stored before they
    are sold

11. the temperature from which all other temperatures are
    measured, usually that at which water freezes

12. a shape like a stretched-out circle

13. a small open building where magazines, candy, and other
    such items are sold

15

WORD LIST 4

denim	habit	rodeo
florist	junk	sculptor
frustrate	local	tenant

denim—(noun) a heavy cotton cloth that can take a lot of hard wear: *Jeans and other work clothes are often made of blue denim.*

florist—(noun) a person who grows or sells flowers for a living: *The florist's shop is at 83 East Seventh Street, next to the drug store.*

frustrate—(verb) to keep someone from doing what he or she wants or needs to do: *His lack of money will frustrate his plans to travel across the country this summer.*

habit—(noun) **1.** something a person does over and over without thinking about it: *Biting your fingernails is a hard habit to break.* **2.** special clothing worn by certain kinds of people: *From the peaked cap to the polished boots, her new riding habit was perfect.*

junk—(noun) anything useless that should be thrown away: *We loaded the truck with junk and took it to the dump.*—(verb) to get rid of something useless: *I will junk my old car this weekend after I get a new one.*

local—(adjective) **1.** having to do with a certain town or place: *You can buy just about anything at the local stores.* **2.** making many stops: *The nonstop train to New York takes two hours, but the local train takes almost three hours.*

rodeo—(noun) a contest or show in which cowboys ride bucking horses and do other such things to show off their skill: *The next event at the rodeo is catching and tying up a young bull.*

sculptor—(noun) an artist who cuts or shapes stone, wood, or clay into shapes meant to be pleasing to the eye: *The sculptor spent long hours in his studio getting his work ready for a show at the art gallery.*

tenant—(noun) a person who pays rent to live in or use the property of another person: *The landlady collects the rent from the tenant each month.*

EXERCISE 4A

Some of the sentences below are true and some are false. On the line to the left of each sentence, write _T_ if you think the sentence is true, and _F_ if you think the sentence is false.

_____ 1. Denim is anything useless that should be thrown away.

_____ 2. Denim is heavy cotton cloth that can take a lot of hard wear.

_____ 3. A florist is a person who grows flowers for a living.

_____ 4. A florist is a person who sells flowers for a living.

_____ 5. To frustrate is to fill up with useless things or ideas.

_____ 6. To frustrate is to keep someone from doing what he or she wants or needs to do.

_____ 7. A habit is special clothing worn by certain kinds of people.

_____ 8. A habit is something a person does over and over without thinking about it.

_____ 9. To junk something is to get rid of it because it is useless.

_____ 10. Junk is anything useless that should be thrown away.

_____ 11. Local means having to do with a certain town or place.

_____ 12. Local means making many stops.

_____ 13. A rodeo is a person who pays rent to live in or use the property of another person.

_____ 14. A rodeo is a contest or show in which cowboys show off their skill.

_____ 15. A sculptor is something cut or shaped which is meant to be pleasing to the eye.

_____ 16. A sculptor is a person who cuts or shapes stone, wood, or clay into shapes meant to be pleasing to the eye.

_____ 17. A tenant is a thin, flat block with writing on it.

_____ 18. A tenant is a person who pays rent to live in or use the property of another person.

Check your answers against the correct ones below. They are not in order. This is to prevent your eye from catching sight of the correct answers before you have had a chance to do the exercise on your own.

14 T.	18 T.	5 F.	11 T.	1 F.	16 T.	10 T.	3 T.	13 F.
8 T.	2 T.	7 T.	12 T.	17 F.	6 T.	15 F.	9 T.	4 T.

EXERCISE 4B

Rewrite each sentence below. Replace the underlined words with the correct vocabulary word from Word List 4.

1. She wore a skirt made of white <u>cotton cloth that can take a lot of hard wear.</u>

   _____

   _____

2. Because this newspaper is <u>sold only in and around this town,</u> it costs very little to advertise in it.

   _____

   _____

3. On our trip out West we plan to see a <u>contest in which cowboys ride bucking horses and do other things to show off their skill.</u>

   _____

   _____

4. This cart with the missing wheels is just a piece of <u>trash that should be thrown away.</u>

   _____

   _____

5. Tell the <u>person who pays rent to live in the apartment</u> that she will be charged fifty dollars more per month, starting April 1.

   _____

   _____

6. He always interrupts people, and that <u>doing it over and over without thinking about it</u> is hard to stop.

   _____

   _____

7. The <u>person who cuts or shapes stone, wood, or clay into pleasing shapes</u> said it took her a year to make the statue of Martin Luther King.

   _____

   _____

8. I bought my grandmother some daisies from the <u>person who sells flowers on the corner.</u>

   _____

   _____

EXERCISE 4C

In the boxes next to each definition, write the correct vocabulary word from Word List 4.
Put one letter in each box. If you do this properly, the long boxes running from top to bottom
will answer the following riddle:

What is the best way to keep lettuce?

1. a contest or show in which cowboys ride bucking horses
   and do other things to show off their skill

2. a person who grows or sells flowers for a living

3. anything useless that should be thrown away

4. special clothing worn by certain kinds of people

5. having to do with a certain place or town

6. to get rid of something useless

7. a person who pays rent to live in or use the property of another

8. heavy cotton cloth that can take a lot of hard wear

9. to keep someone from doing what he or she wants
   or needs to do

10. something a person does over and over without thinking
    about it

11. making many stops

12. a person who cuts or shapes stone, wood, or clay into
    shapes meant to be pleasing to the eye

CROSSWORD 2

Decide what word from Word List 3 or 4 is missing from each sentence below. For the first group of sentences (Clues Across), write each answer in the boxes running across on the puzzle on the next page. For the second group (Clues Down), write each answer in the boxes running down.

Work out the sentences in any order you like; just be sure to match the number of the sentence with the number in the box. Put only one letter in each box. If all your answers are correct, all the words on the puzzle will fit together.

Clues Across

2. She opened a folder and took out a thick _____ of papers.

5. Put that sofa with the broken springs in the spare room with the other _____.

8. We rowed out to the small _____ in the middle of the lake.

9. He loves flowers and wants to train to be a _____ when he leaves school.

10. The number *10* is made up of the number for *one* followed by a _____.

11. It will cost too much to repair the TV set, so we will _____ it.

13. These country children attend the _____ school until eighth grade, and after that, they go to school in the city.

15. _____ the meat into bite-sized pieces before you cook it.

16. The lizard is a _____ which can range in length from two inches to ten feet.

19. The lowest temperature ever recorded in the United States was eighty degrees below

    _____ at Prospect Creek, Alaska.

20. The town of Pompeii was buried when the _____ known as Mt. Vesuvius erupted.

22. I was _____ for school this morning because I missed the bus.

23. Are you a _____, or do you own your house?

Clues Down

1. The nun who teaches first grade wears a black _____.

3. His _____ of humming at his desk bothered the other workers.

4. The _____ is popular in the American West.

6. The sidewalk by the _____ was littered with candy wrappers.

7. The van left the _____ with a load of beds and mattresses.

9. He refused to let his deafness _____ him in his drive to get good grades.

12. The faces of four presidents were carved on Mount Rushmore by the _____ Gutzon Borglum.

13. Set your alarm clock if you don't want to be _____.

14. The farmer's overalls were blue _____ and his shirt red wool.

17. Take the _____ bus if you're not in a big hurry.

18. The funeral for the _____ president will be held on Thursday.

21. A plate looked at from the side seems to be _____.

WORD LIST 5

appetite   crow   mental
barometer dent   wisp
code   granite

appetite—(noun) a desire or wish to eat food: *The hike we took gave us an appetite for lunch.*

barometer—(noun) an instrument that measures changes in air pressure. It is used to tell the kind of weather we can expect: *When the needle on the barometer shows a drop in the air pressure, the weather usually turns wet and windy.*

code—(noun) **1.** a method of writing or sending messages so that they cannot be understood just by looking at them: *By using certain numbers in place of letters, you can write in code.* **2.** a set of rules that tells how to act or behave: *The new dress code does not allow students to wear jeans or sneakers.*

crow—(noun) **1.** a large black bird with a harsh, cawing cry: *The crow builds its nest high up in tall trees.* **2.** the sound that a rooster makes: *The crow of the rooster is the first sound of the morning on the farm.*—(verb) to make the sound of a rooster: *When a rooster crows, it stretches its neck up.*

dent—(noun) a hollow place in a hard surface like metal that is made by its being struck: *Be careful when you knock out the dent in that pot.*—(verb) to hit a hard surface like metal and make a hollow place there: *Did you dent the truck's fender when you backed into it?*

granite—(noun) a very hard rock of a speckled gray-pink color that can be cut into blocks and used for building: *The surface of granite can be made smooth and polished to show off its color.*

mental—(adjective) having to do with the mind: *Mental arithmetic is done in the head without using pencil and paper.*

wisp—(noun) **1.** a small bunch or tuft of something like hair or hay: *She tucked a little wisp of hair back under her ski cap.* **2.** a puff or tiny cloud: *A wisp of smoke from the damp twigs showed that she had finally started the fire.*

EXERCISE 5A

Some of the sentences below are true and some are false. On the line to the left of each sentence, write _T_ if you think the sentence is true, and _F_ if you think the sentence is false.

_____ 1. An appetite is a desire or wish for food.

_____ 2. An appetite is something to eat between meals.

_____ 3. A barometer measures changes in air pressure.

_____ 4. A barometer tells us what the weather is likely to be.

_____ 5. A code is a set of rules that tells how to act or behave.

_____ 6. A code is a method of writing that cannot be understood just by looking at it.

_____ 7. A crow is a large black bird with a harsh, cawing cry.

_____ 8. To crow is to make the sound of a rooster.

_____ 9. A dent is a small bunch or tuft of something like hair or hay.

_____ 10. To dent is to hit a hard surface like metal and make a hollow place there.

_____ 11. Granite is a heavy cotton cloth that can take a lot of hard wear.

_____ 12. Granite is a very hard rock of a speckled gray-pink color.

_____ 13. Mental means having to do with the mind.

_____ 14. Mental means having to do with the body.

_____ 15. A wisp is a puff or tiny cloud.

_____ 16. A wisp is a small bunch or tuft of something like hair or hay.

Check your answers against the correct ones below. They are not in order. This is to prevent your eye from catching sight of the correct answers before you have had a chance to do the exercise on your own.

4 T.	11 F.	16 T.	1 T.	12 T.	6 T.	2 F.	10 T.
15 T.	9 F.	3 T.	7 T.	14 F.	5 T.	8 T.	13 T.

EXERCISE 5B

Rewrite each sentence below. Replace the underlined words with the correct vocabulary word from Word List 5.

1. She was a good spy because she could often read messages sent in <u>a method of writing that cannot be understood just by looking at it.</u>

   _____

   _____

2. The sailor looked at the <u>instrument that shows changes in air pressure</u> and got ready for a storm.

   _____

   _____

3. A sick person usually has very little <u>desire to eat food.</u>

   _____

   _____

4. You made that <u>hollow place</u> in the car when you hit that block of <u>very hard, speckled gray and pink rock.</u>

   _____

   _____

5. Work that is <u>done by the mind</u> can be very tiring.

   _____

   _____

6. A <u>puff or tiny cloud</u> of smoke came from the gun barrel.

   _____

   _____

7. The <u>set of rules that tells people how to behave</u> at the school does not allow cheating.

   _____

   _____

8. The <u>large black bird with the harsh, cawing cry</u> flew away as we got nearer to it.

   _____

   _____

EXERCISE 5C

In the boxes next to each definition, write the correct vocabulary word from Word List 5.
Put one letter in each box. If you do this properly, the long boxes running from top to bottom
will answer the following riddle:

What did Silly Billy miss most when he went to the city?

1. a desire or wish for food

2. a way of writing or sending messages that cannot be understood just by looking at it

3. a very hard rock of a speckled gray-pink color that can be cut into blocks and used for building

4. a small bunch or tuft of something like hair or hay

5. a hollow place in a hard surface like metal that is made by its being hit

6. having to do with the mind

7. a large black bird with a harsh, cawing cry

8. a puff or tiny cloud of something

9. to hit against a hard surface and make a hollow place there

10. to make the sound of a rooster

11. an instrument used to measure changes in air pressure

12. a set of rules that tells how to act or behave

WORD LIST 6

adopt   discard   owe
dairy   drowsy   pang
detour   grain   traitor

adopt—(verb) **1.** to take into a family as a son or daughter: *They have two children already and will soon adopt a third.* **2.** to take up and use or follow: *The school will adopt the new dress code on January 1.*

dairy—(noun) **1.** a place where milk and cream are made into butter, cheese, and other milk products: *The truck from the dairy delivers fresh milk to the stores every day.* **2.** a farm where cows are kept to give milk: *The dairy has over two hundred cows.* **3.** a store that sells milk and milk products: *The dairy at the corner stays open twenty-four hours a day.*

detour—(noun) a turning aside from the usual way of going: *We had to take a detour because the road ahead was flooded.*—(verb) to turn aside from the usual way of going: *Cars must detour ahead because the road is being repaired.*

discard—(verb) to throw away or get rid of: *You can discard these old drawings since no one wants them.*

drowsy—(adjective) sleepy; about to fall asleep: *If you become drowsy while driving, you should pull off the road and rest.*

grain—(noun) **1.** the small, hard seed of cereal plants such as corn and wheat: *Each grain of corn is puffed up by heat to make popcorn.* **2.** a single tiny piece of something: *Even a few grains of spilled sugar may attract ants during the summer.* **3.** the markings or pattern on the surface of wood formed by the rings that make up the tree: *By looking at the grain, you can tell what kind of tree the wood is from.*

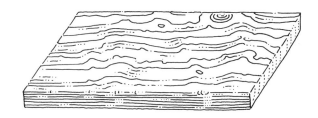

owe—(verb) **1.** to have a debt to someone: *When will you repay the ten dollars you owe me?* **2.** to feel a need to do something in return for what has been done: *We owe a lot to the people who work for the Red Cross without pay.*

pang—(noun) a sudden, sharp pain or feeling: *I felt a pang of sorrow when I had to leave my family.*

traitor—(noun) a person who helps the enemy of his or her country: *Benedict Arnold was an American traitor who helped the British when they were fighting his country.*

EXERCISE 6A

Some of the sentences below are true and some are false. On the line to the left of each sentence, write _T_ if you think the sentence is true, and _F_ if you think the sentence is false.

_____ 1. To adopt is to take into a family as a son or daughter.

_____ 2. To adopt is to take up and use or follow.

_____ 3. A dairy is a farm where cows are kept to give milk.

_____ 4. A dairy is a store where milk and milk products are sold.

_____ 5. A detour is a sudden, sharp pain or feeling.

_____ 6. A detour is a turning aside from the usual way of going.

_____ 7. To discard is to keep someone from doing what he or she wants to do.

_____ 8. To discard is to throw away or get rid of.

_____ 9. Drowsy means about to fall asleep.

_____ 10. Drowsy means having no wish for food.

_____ 11. Grain is the small, hard seed of cereal plants such as corn and wheat.

_____ 12. A grain is a single tiny piece of something.

_____ 13. To owe is to have to pay back what has been borrowed.

_____ 14. To owe is to feel a need to do something in return for what has been done.

_____ 15. A pang is a sudden, sharp pain or feeling.

_____ 16. A pang is the small, hard seed of cereal plants like corn or wheat.

_____ 17. A traitor is a person who is willing to fight for his or her country against its enemies.

_____ 18. A traitor is a person who helps the enemy of his or her country.

Check your answers against the correct ones below. They are not in order. This is to prevent your eye from catching sight of the correct answers before you have had a chance to do the exercise on your own.

| 13 T. | 1 T. | 6 T. | 10 F. | 3 T. | 14 T. | 7 F. | 11 T. | 18 T. |
| 12 T. | 4 T. | 2 T. | 16 F. | 9 T. | 5 F. | 15 T. | 8 T. | 17 F. |

EXERCISE 6B

Rewrite each sentence below. Replace the underlined words with the correct vocabulary word from Word List 6.

1. He will <u>get rid of</u> this piece of wood because he does not like the <u>pattern on the surface made by the tree's rings.</u>

   _____

   _____

2. I thought they were <u>about to fall asleep,</u> so I suggested going to bed.

   _____

   _____

3. They will <u>take into their family as their son</u> the little boy whose parents died.

   _____

   _____

4. It is impossible to count every <u>single tiny piece</u> of sand on the beach.

   _____

   _____

5. If we <u>turn aside from the usual way of going,</u> it will add five miles to the trip.

   _____

   _____

6. If you didn't borrow any money, then you don't <u>have to pay back</u> anything.

   _____

   _____

7. The <u>person who had helped the enemy of her country</u> felt a <u>sudden sharp feeling</u> of guilt when she thought about what she had done.

   _____

   _____

8. Our class took a trip to the <u>place where milk and cream are made into milk products.</u>

   _____

   _____

EXERCISE 6C

In the boxes next to each definition, write the correct vocabulary word from Word List 6.
Put one letter in each box. If you do this properly, the long boxes running from top to bottom
will answer the following riddle:

Why doesn't a bull give milk?

1. a person who helps the enemy of his or her country

2. to turn aside from the usual way of going

3. the markings or pattern on the surface of wood formed by the rings that make up the tree

   l

4. to have to pay back what has been borrowed

5. the small, hard seed of cereal plants like wheat or corn

6. a farm where cows are kept to give milk

7. sleepy; about to fall asleep

8. to throw away or get rid of

   h

9. to take up and use or follow

10. a single tiny piece of something

11. a sudden, sharp pain or feeling

12. to feel a need to do something in return for what has been done

    s

13. a place where milk and cream are made into butter, cheese, and other milk products

    o

    u.

CROSSWORD 3

Decide what word from Word List 5 or 6 is missing from each sentence below. For the first group of sentences (Clues Across), write each answer in the boxes running across on the puzzle on the next page. For the second group (Clues Down), write each answer in the boxes running down.

Work out the sentences in any order you like; just be sure to match the number of the sentence with the number in the box. Put only one letter in each box. If all your answers are correct, all the words on the puzzle will fit together.

Clues Across

3. The _____ sells yogurt in ten flavors.

5. The old stove works well although it has a few scratches and a big _____ in the door.

8. The sign in the store window said, "Fresh milk from the _____."

9. I felt a _____ of hunger when I smelled the bread baking.

11. _____ illness is sometimes difficult to treat.

14. To build the highway, the workers had to blast big chunks of _____ out of the hillside.

16. The _____ of straw in the bird's beak showed that it was building its nest.

17. Of the seven cards you are dealt in this game, you keep five and _____ two.

20. I _____ my grandfather a letter; it has been a month since he wrote to me.

21. The _____ we had to make took us through some pretty country roads.

22. In Morse _____ the letter *V* is written ...– .

23. The sky was clear except for a _____ of cloud very high up.

24. Figure out how much I _____ you, and I will write you a check.

Clues Down

1. Before you can _____ a baby, you have to prove you will be a good parent.

2. I was awakened by the _____ of the rooster at 5:00 A.M.

4. We will _____ the new rule for the time being to see how it works out.

6. When the _____ is rising, it means that fair weather is coming.

7. He put a _____ or two of the white stuff on his tongue and said that it was salt.

10. The prairies of the American Midwest grow the finest _____ in the world.

12. "Yes," he said, "I did pass secrets to the enemy, but I am not a _____."

13. We stripped the paint off the wooden table to show off the _____.

15. She looked at the burned food and said she had lost her _____.

18. Being careful with matches should be part of the _____ of those who visit our national forests.

19. He said, "I feel _____," after he had lain in the hot sun for an hour.

22. A scare_____ is set up in a field to frighten away the birds.

WORD LIST 7

cue   ornament   whittle
cymbal   perish   yard
murmur   unicorn

cue—(noun) **1.** a long stick, thin at one end, used to strike the ball in pool and other games: *You hold the cue by the thick end and aim the thin end between the fingers of your other hand.* **2.** the last words of an actor's speech that tell the next actor when to say or do whatever comes next: *Her words "I love you" are the cue for him to kiss her.* **3.** a signal to do something: *The ringing of the school bell is not a cue for everyone to rush for the door.* —(verb) to give a sign or signal that it is time to do something: *She will cue the singers to begin by dropping her arm suddenly.*

cymbal—(noun) a round brass plate that makes a ringing sound when struck: *The piece of music ended with a great crash of one cymbal against another.*

murmur—(noun) a low, steady sound: *I lay in bed and listened to the murmur of the wind in the trees.*—(verb) **1.** to make low, steady sounds: *The bees murmur as they go from flower to flower.* **2.** to speak in a low voice: *I heard her murmur something in his ear.*

ornament—(noun) anything that is put somewhere just to be looked at and admired: *We carefully hung each shiny ornament on the Christmas tree.*

perish—(verb) to die, especially as a result of some great misfortune: *Many animals perish in a forest fire.*

unicorn—(noun) an animal that is not real, but that is supposed to look like a white horse with one straight horn in the middle of its forehead: *Although the unicorn is not real, it is fun to read about and draw.*

whittle—(verb) **1.** to make little cuts in wood: *The old man would often whittle on a stick just to pass the time.* **2.** to make less and less, a little at a time: *We whittled down the cost of fixing up the new house by doing many of the jobs ourselves.*

yard—(noun) **1.** a measure of length that is equal to three feet or thirty-six inches: *You will need another yard of cloth to make a curtain for this window.* **2.** the land next to a house or other building: *The house has a big yard where we can set up the swing set.* **3.** a place where certain kinds of work or business are done: *We get our wood from the local lumber yard.*

EXERCISE 7A

Some of the sentences below are true and some are false. On the line to the left of each sentence, write _T_ if you think the sentence is true, and _F_ if you think the sentence is false.

_____ 1. A cue is a signal to do something.

_____ 2. A cue is a long stick used to hit the ball in the game of pool.

_____ 3. A cymbal is an animal that isn't real, but that is supposed to look like a white horse with a straight horn in the middle of its forehead.

_____ 4. A cymbal is a round brass plate that makes a ringing sound when struck.

_____ 5. A murmur is a low, steady sound.

_____ 6. To murmur is to say something in a low voice.

_____ 7. An ornament is a measure of length equal to thirty-six inches.

_____ 8. An ornament is anything that is put somewhere just to be looked at and admired.

_____ 9. To perish is to make little cuts in wood.

_____ 10. To perish is to die, especially as a result of some great misfortune.

_____ 11. A unicorn is not real but is found only in things like books and paintings.

_____ 12. A unicorn is supposed to look like a white horse with a single horn in the middle of its forehead.

_____ 13. To whittle is to turn aside from the usual way of going.

_____ 14. To whittle is to make less and less, a little at a time.

_____ 15. A yard is the land next to a house or other building.

_____ 16. A yard is a measure of length equal to three feet.

Check your answers against the correct ones below. They are not in order. This is to prevent your eye from catching sight of the correct answers before you have had a chance to do the exercise on your own.

5 T.	10 T.	15 T.	2 T.	12 T.	6 T.	11 T.	8 T.
16 T.	3 F.	9 F.	1 T.	13 F.	7 F.	4 T.	14 T.

EXERCISE 7B

Rewrite each sentence below. Replace the underlined words with the correct vocabulary word from Word List 7.

1. As he left the room, I heard him <u>say in a low voice</u> that life isn't fair.

   _____

   _____

2. Many people will <u>die as a result of a great misfortune</u> if they are not warned that an earthquake is due.

   _____

   _____

3. She has a job at the boat <u>place where work is done</u> mending sails.

   _____

   _____

4. The old clock doesn't work, but we keep it as an <u>object just to be looked at and admired.</u>

   _____

   _____

5. She can <u>make little cuts in</u> a hollow stick and turn it into a kind of flute.

   _____

   _____

6. The <u>stick used to strike the ball in the game of pool</u> has a rubber tip at the thin end.

   _____

   _____

7. "Goodbye" is the <u>last word of the actor's speech</u> that tells you when to say your lines.

   _____

   _____

8. You hold each <u>round brass plate that makes a ringing sound</u> by the leather strap on the back.

   _____

   _____

EXERCISE 7C

In the boxes next to each definition, write the correct vocabulary word from Word List 7. Put one letter in each box. If you do this properly, the long boxes running from top to bottom will answer the following riddle:

What did Silly Milly do with the flypaper?

1. to make low, steady sounds

2. anything that is put somewhere just to be looked at and admired

3. a unit of length equal to three feet or thirty-six inches

4. the last words of an actor's speech that tell the next actor when to say or do what comes next

5. the land next to a house or other building

6. to die, especially as a result of some great misfortune

7. to make little cuts in wood

8. to give a sign or signal that it is time to do something

9. a place where certain kinds of business or work are done

10. a round brass plate that makes a ringing sound when struck

11. an animal that is not real, but that is supposed to look like a white horse with a straight horn in the middle of its forehead

12. to make less and less, a little at a time

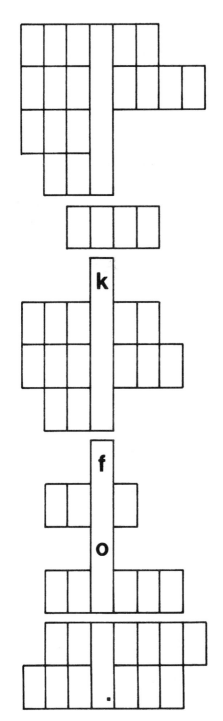

35

WORD LIST 8

bait	magic	prod
hutch	margin	straddle
luxury	mascot	

bait—(noun) food that is used to attract and catch fish and some kinds of animals: *Cheese is the best bait for catching mice.*—(verb) **1.** to attach food to a hook or trap in order to catch fish or animals: *Bait the hook with a worm before you toss it into the water.* **2.** to tease or torment: *They baited the little boy by grabbing his cap and tossing it into the air.*

hutch—(noun) **1.** a box with wire netting across its front in which rabbits and other small animals are kept: *Someone left the hutch door open, and the rabbits escaped.* **2.** a piece of furniture used to hold things like glasses and dishes: *The hutch has three shelves, a drawer, and two doors at the bottom.*

luxury—(noun) something that costs a lot of money and is wanted but not really needed: *Jane's mother said a new stereo set was a luxury, but Jane said she really needed it.*

magic—(noun) **1.** a strange power to do things not usually possible: *The Fairy Godmother used magic to turn a pumpkin into a coach.* **2.** the use of tricks on stage to fool people into thinking that something strange has happened: *The finest bit of magic she did was to saw through a box with a man inside without hurting him.*

margin—(noun) **1.** the empty space around the written or printed area on a page: *A wide margin makes a page less crowded and easier to read.* **2.** an extra amount of something like time or money: *I need ten dollars and am taking fifteen, so that leaves a margin of five dollars.*

mascot—(noun) a person, animal, or thing that is supposed to bring good luck: *The football team's mascot is a bulldog, a fierce-looking animal.*

prod—(noun) **1.** a stick used to jab or poke with: *The animals won't move back to the barn unless you use a prod on them.* **2.** a jab or poke with something: *She gave me a prod in the ribs with her finger.*—(verb) to keep pushing or urging someone to do something: *Usually Karl enjoys playing the piano, but sometimes we must prod him to practice.*

straddle—(verb) to stand or sit with a leg on either side of something: *In this exercise, you straddle the bar and then spin around it.*

EXERCISE 8A

Some of the sentences below are true and some are false. On the line to the left of each sentence, write *T* if you think the sentence is true, and *F* if you think the sentence is false.

_____ 1. To bait is to attach food to a hook or trap in order to catch fish or some kinds of animals.

_____ 2. To bait is to tease or torment.

_____ 3. A hutch is a piece of furniture used to hold things like glasses and dishes.

_____ 4. A hutch is a box with wire netting across the front in which small animals are kept.

_____ 5. A luxury is a person, animal, or thing that is supposed to bring good luck.

_____ 6. A luxury is something that costs a lot of money and is wanted but not really needed.

_____ 7. Magic is a strange power to do things not usually possible.

_____ 8. Magic is the use of tricks on stage to fool people into thinking something strange has happened.

_____ 9. A margin is the empty space around the written or printed area on a page.

_____ 10. A margin is an extra amount of something like time or money.

_____ 11. A mascot is a round brass plate that makes a ringing noise when struck.

_____ 12. A mascot is a person, animal, or thing that is supposed to bring good luck.

_____ 13. A prod is a stick used to jab or poke with.

_____ 14. A prod is a jab or poke with something.

_____ 15. To straddle is to make a low, steady sound.

_____ 16. To straddle is to stand or sit with a leg on either side of something.

Check your answers against the correct ones below. They are not in order. This is to prevent your eye from catching sight of the correct answers before you have had a chance to do the exercise on your own.

10 T.	2 T.	6 T.	13 T.	16 T.	7 T.	3 T.	12 T.
9 T.	4 T.	1 T.	15 F.	8 T.	11 F.	14 T.	5 F.

EXERCISE 8B

Rewrite each sentence below. Replace the underlined words with the correct vocabulary word from Word List 8.

1. We didn't need to <u>keep urging and pushing</u> Betsy to do her homework.

_____

_____

2. As I was reading the math book, I made a few notes in the <u>empty space around the printed area on the page.</u>

_____

_____

3. Many people would call a movie camera a <u>thing that may be wanted but not really needed.</u>

_____

_____

4. The stuffed bear was the team's <u>thing that was supposed to bring good luck.</u>

_____

_____

5. Can you do <u>tricks on stage that fool people into thinking that something strange has happened?</u>

_____

_____

6. Put some clean straw in the <u>box with the wire netting across the front where small animals are kept.</u>

_____

_____

7. Did you see him <u>sit with a leg on either side of</u> the fence?

_____

_____

8. To get the sheep through the gate, the rancher needed a <u>stick used for poking.</u>

_____

_____

EXERCISE 8C

In the boxes next to each definition, write the correct vocabulary word from Word List 8. Put one letter in each box. If you do this properly, the long boxes running from top to bottom will answer the following riddle:

Why did the horse fly?

1. a strange power to do things not usually possible

2. food that is used to attract and catch fish and some kinds of animals

3. a person, animal, or thing that is supposed to bring good luck

4. the empty space around the written or printed area on a page

5. a piece of furniture used to hold things like glasses and dishes

6. a box with wire netting across its front in which rabbits and other small animals are kept

7. to stand or sit with a leg on either side of something

8. a jab or poke with something

9. to tease or torment

10. the use of tricks on stage to fool people into thinking something strange has happened

11. to keep pushing or urging someone to do something

12. an extra amount of something like money or time

13. something that costs a lot of money and is wanted but not really needed

39

CROSSWORD 4

Decide what word from Word List 7 or 8 is missing from each sentence below. For the first group of sentences (Clues Across), write each answer in the boxes running across on the puzzle on the next page. For the second group (Clues Down), write each answer in the boxes running down.

Work out the sentences in any order you like; just be sure to match the number of the sentence with the number in the box. Put only one letter in each box. If all your answers are correct, all the words on the puzzle will fit together.

Clues Across

2. She had millions of dollars and could afford every _____ that she wanted.

7. Some of the pictures in the book go right to the edge of the page and leave no _____.

8. A cattle _____ gives a small electric shock to the cow poked with it.

11. It takes an hour to drive to the airport, and your plane leaves in an hour, so we have no

   _____ of time.

12. The _____ to kill the rats is bread with poison on it.

13. He started to yell at us, so we took that as our _____ to leave.

15. Women once rode sidesaddle, and so their legs did not _____ the horse.

16. We built a _____ in the garden for the hamsters to live in during the summer.

18. When the great rivers of India go over their banks, thousands of people _____
   in the floods.

21. I heard her _____ something, but I could not tell exactly what she said.

22. Eighteen inches is the same as half a _____.

23. Before going onto the field, he touched the _____ for good luck.

Clues Down

1. The first actor says, "Excuse me," and that is your _____ to leave.

3. The word _____ comes from two Latin words meaning "one horn."

4. The train's broken front light was fixed in the railroad _____.

5. The only _____ on the shelf was a small china dog.

6. The owners of the business will _____ down their costs by hiring fewer
   summer workers.

7. You have to practice your tricks carefully before you do your _____ on stage.

9. I watched my grandfather take a block of wood and _____ a bird out of it.

10. The large family wanted a big _____ where the children could play outdoors.

14. The witch in the story used _____ to turn the two boys into mice.

17. Sometimes a _____ is fastened to a drum and struck with a drumstick.

18. She's never hungry, so we must _____ her to eat.

19. The knives and forks are kept in the drawer of the _____.

20. The older children _____ the younger ones by snatching away their toys.

WORD LIST 9

barge   fleece   surf
diamond   gray   tomahawk
ember   locket   tutor
portrait

barge—(noun) a large flat boat pulled over water and used for carrying goods: *The tugboat pulled the barge filled with coal.* —(verb) to enter in a clumsy or rude way: *Don't barge in and start giving orders where you are not wanted.*

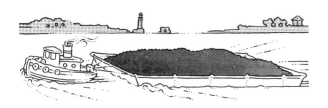

diamond—(noun) **1.** a four-sided figure of this shape ◊: *The infield at a baseball park is shaped like a diamond with a base at each of its four corners.* **2.** a very hard stone that can be cut and polished and used as a jewel: *A well-cut diamond flashes and sparkles as it is turned in the light.*

ember—(noun) a piece of wood or coal still burning in a fire that is almost out: *One ember was still glowing, and I blew on it to try to get the fire started again.*

fleece—(noun) the coat of wool on a sheep or goat: *In cold lands the sheep grow a thicker and warmer fleece.* —(verb) **1.** to cut off all the wool from a sheep or goat: *The sheep farmers fleece the sheep in spring, and in the fall, the wool grows again.* **2.** to take money from by cheating or tricking: *She fleeced him of the money he gave her to take care of.*

gray—(adjective) **1.** a color that is a mix of black and white: *Tiny black and white dots close together will seem gray when looked at from a distance.* **2.** dull or depressing: *Some people think a rainy day is gray, but I love the rain.*

locket—(noun) a small metal case that opens to show a picture. It is usually worn from a necklace: *When her necklace broke, the locket fell to the floor and snapped open.*

portrait—(noun) **1.** a photograph, drawing, or painting of a person, especially one showing the face: *A portrait of Mother Teresa of Calcutta hangs in the lobby of the school.* **2.** a piece of writing that tells what a person is like: *The portrait of Joshua in the first chapter stays in one's mind through the whole book.*

surf—(noun) the waves of the sea as they reach the shore and break up: *The crashing surf knocked her down, but she got up laughing.* —(verb) to ride the waves on a board: *Marie wants to learn how to surf.*

tomahawk—(noun) a light ax once used by Native Americans as a tool for cutting and as a weapon for fighting: *When it was thrown with skill, the tomahawk could be a deadly weapon.*

tutor—(noun) a person who teaches in private and not in the classroom: *She needs a tutor this summer to help her with French.* —(verb) to teach in private rather than in the classroom: *He will tutor the students who want to improve their math scores.*

42

EXERCISE 9A

Some of the sentences below are true and some are false. On the line to the left of each sentence, write _T_ if you think the sentence is true, and _F_ if you think the sentence is false.

_____ 1. To barge in is to teach in private rather than in the classroom.

_____ 2. To barge in is to enter in a rude or clumsy way.

_____ 3. A diamond is a very hard stone.

_____ 4. A diamond is a four-sided figure like this ◇.

_____ 5. An ember is a light ax once used by Native Americans.

_____ 6. An ember is a piece of wood still burning in a fire that is almost out.

_____ 7. To fleece is to take money from by cheating or tricking.

_____ 8. To fleece is to cut off all the wool from a sheep or goat.

_____ 9. Gray is a color made by mixing black and white.

_____ 10. Gray means dull or depressing.

_____ 11. A locket is a large flat boat that is pulled over water.

_____ 12. A locket is a small metal case that opens to show a picture.

_____ 13. A portrait is a picture of a person, especially one showing the face.

_____ 14. A portrait is a piece of writing that describes a person.

_____ 15. Surf is the coat of wool on a sheep or goat.

_____ 16. Surf is the waves of the sea as they break up on shore.

_____ 17. A tomahawk is something that is believed to bring good luck.

_____ 18. A tomahawk is a light ax once used by Native Americans.

_____ 19. To tutor is to teach in private rather than in public.

_____ 20. To tutor is to take money from by cheating or tricking.

Check your answers against the correct ones below. They are not in order. This is to prevent your eye from catching sight of the correct answers before you have had a chance to do the exercise on your own.

17 F.	13 T.	3 T.	9 T.	20 F.	15 F.	1 F.	7 T.	18 T.	14 T.
11 F.	2 T.	5 F.	19 T.	10 T.	4 T.	12 T.	16 T.	6 T.	8 T.

43

EXERCISE 9B

Rewrite each sentence below. Replace the underlined words with the correct vocabulary word from Word List 9.

1. The <u>large flat boat used to carry goods</u> was painted <u>a color that is a mix of black and white.</u>

   _____

   _____

2. Just to be safe, he pulled the last <u>piece of wood still burning</u> from the fire.

   _____

   _____

3. The <u>light ax once used by Native Americans</u> is so sharp it can <u>cut off all the wool from</u> a sheep.

   _____

   _____

4. Inside the <u>small metal case that hung from her necklace</u> was a <u>picture showing the face</u> of her mother.

   _____

   _____

5. It's fun to play in the <u>waves that break on the shore.</u>

   _____

   _____

6. The <u>person who is hired to teach privately</u> should be paid by the hour.

   _____

   _____

7. The burglar escaped with a <u>small, hard stone, cut and polished and used as a jewel</u> and a pair of earrings.

   _____

   _____

8. I knew the big kids would <u>clumsily and rudely enter</u> in and spoil our fun.

   _____

   _____

EXERCISE 9C

In the boxes next to each definition, write the correct vocabulary word from Word List 9.
Put one letter in each box. If you do this properly, the long boxes running from top to bottom
will answer the following riddle:

Why is an egg like a losing team?

1. to enter in a crude or clumsy way

2. a very hard stone that can be cut and polished and used as a jewel

3. a picture of a person, especially one showing the face

4. a light ax once used by Native Americans as a tool for cutting and a weapon for fighting

5. a large flat boat pulled over water and used for carrying goods

6. the waves of the sea as they reach the shore and break up

7. to take money from by cheating or tricking

8. a piece of wood or coal still burning in a fire that is almost out

9. the coat of wool of a sheep or goat

10. a mix of black and white

11. to teach in private rather than in a classroom

12. a small metal case that opens to show a picture

13. a four-sided figure of this shape ◇

45

WORD LIST 10

beeline	evacuate	sift
clang	foe	steam
eavesdrop	moat	wedge
	profile	

beeline—(noun) a line that goes straight from one place to another: *As soon as Johnny walks in the door, he makes a beeline for the refrigerator.*

clang—(noun) the sound made by metal that is struck: *The clapper strikes the inside of the bell and that makes a loud clang.*—(verb) to make a sound of metal being struck: *He felt scared when he heard the steel door of his prison cell clang shut.*

eavesdrop—(verb) to listen secretly to what someone else is saying: *He eavesdropped on his parents and learned what they were planning to give him for his birthday.*

evacuate—(verb) to move out of danger: *We must evacuate the people of the town if the river floods its banks.*

foe—(noun) an enemy; something or someone who tries to harm another: *Japan was once the foe of the United States, but now the two countries are friends.*

moat—(noun) a deep ditch dug around a castle and filled with water to make it harder to attack the castle: *People could enter and leave the castle only when the drawbridge over the moat was lowered.*

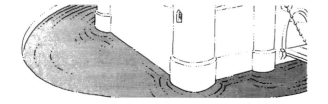

profile—(noun) **1.** a side view of a person's head: *An American quarter has a profile of George Washington on one side.* **2.** anything seen only in outline: *We could just make out the profile of the roof and chimney against the dark sky.*

sift—(verb) **1.** to pass through a strainer in order to separate larger pieces from smaller ones: *Sift out the pebbles from this sand.* **2.** to look through with care: *Sift through the trash and see if you can find the missing bus ticket.*

steam—(noun) **1.** water that has been turned into a white mist by being heated: *You can get a bad burn from the steam from boiling water.* **2.** water that forms a film of tiny drops on cold surfaces: *Steam forms on the windows when they are much colder than the air in the room.*—(verb) **1.** to give off a white mist formed by water being heated: *Water steams when it boils.* **2.** to move, especially by using a steam engine for power: *We watched the ship as it steamed into the harbor.*

wedge—(noun) **1.** a piece of wood or metal that is thick at one end and thin at the other: *The thin end of the wedge is driven deeper when the thick end is struck with a hammer.* **2.** anything of this shape ∇ that is thick at one end and thin at the other: *I cut myself a wedge of cake.*—(verb) **1.** to hold in place with the thin end of something: *Wedge the door open with this piece of wood.* **2.** to pack tightly: *Sixteen people were wedged into the tiny room.*

EXERCISE 10A

Some of the sentences below are true and some are false. On the line to the left of each sentence, write _T_ if you think the sentence is true, and _F_ if you think the sentence is false.

_____ 1. A beeline is a deep ditch dug around a castle and filled with water.

_____ 2. A beeline is a line that goes straight from one place to another.

_____ 3. A clang is the sound made by metal that is struck.

_____ 4. A clang is a piece of metal which is thick at one end and thin at the other.

_____ 5. To eavesdrop is to move out of danger.

_____ 6. To eavesdrop is to listen secretly to what someone else is saying.

_____ 7. To evacuate is to pass through a strainer.

_____ 8. To evacuate is to move out of danger.

_____ 9. A foe is a side view of a person's head.

_____ 10. A foe is an enemy, something or someone who tries to harm another.

_____ 11. A moat is a deep ditch dug around a castle and filled with water.

_____ 12. A moat is a long, narrow groove made by a plow turning over the earth.

_____ 13. A profile is anything seen only in outline.

_____ 14. A profile is a side view of a person's head.

_____ 15. To sift is to pass through a strainer.

_____ 16. To sift is to look through with great care.

_____ 17. To steam is to give off a white mist formed by water being heated.

_____ 18. To steam is to move, especially by using a steam engine for power.

_____ 19. To wedge is to hold in place with the thin end of something.

_____ 20. To wedge is to pack in tightly.

Check your answers against the correct ones below. They are not in order. This is to prevent your eye from catching sight of the correct answers before you have had a chance to do the exercise on your own.

11 T.	17 T.	6 T.	9 F.	15 T.	19 T.	13 T.	3 T.	7 F.	10 T.
12 F.	18 T.	1 F.	5 F.	8 T.	2 T.	16 T.	20 T.	14 T.	4 F.

EXERCISE 10B

Rewrite each sentence below. Replace the underlined words with the correct vocabulary word from Word List 10.

1. Every day after school Marta makes a <u>journey that goes in a straight line</u> for home.

   _____

   _____

2. To split the log, she used a hammer and a <u>piece of metal that is thick at one end and thin at the other.</u>

   _____

   _____

3. The <u>deep ditch filled with water that runs around the castle</u> keeps the <u>people who are trying to do harm</u> from attacking.

   _____

   _____

4. She heard a <u>sound of metal striking metal</u> as the iron gates shut.

   _____

   _____

5. The bathroom was filled with <u>water that had been turned into a white mist</u> after I took my hot shower.

   _____

   _____

6. Su-lin asked her son to turn to the side so she could sketch his <u>side view of the head.</u>

   _____

   _____

7. He will sometimes <u>listen secretly to what others are saying</u> and then tell his buddies what he has heard.

   _____

   _____

8. There is a plan to <u>move out of danger</u> everyone living near the volcano if it erupts again.

   _____

   _____

EXERCISE 10C

In the boxes next to each definition, write the correct vocabulary word from Word List 10. Put one letter in each box. If you do this properly, the long boxes running from top to bottom will answer the following riddle:

How do you get a sleeping gorilla out of your bed?

1. a piece of wood or metal that is thick at one end and thin at the other

2. to make a sound of metal being struck

3. a side view of a person's head

4. to pass through a strainer in order to separate larger pieces from smaller ones

5. an enemy; something or someone who tries to harm another

6. a deep ditch dug around a castle and filled with water to make it harder to attack the castle

7. to listen secretly to what others are saying

8. a line that goes straight from one place to another

9. to move, especially by using a steam engine for power

10. water that forms a film of tiny drops on cold surfaces

11. anything seen only in outline

12. to pack tightly

13. anything of this shape ▽ that is thick at one end and thin at the other

14. to look through with care

15. to move out of danger

49

CROSSWORD 5

Decide what word from Word List 9 or 10 is missing from each sentence below. For the first group of sentences (Clues Across), write each answer in the boxes running across on the puzzle on the next page. For the second group (Clues Down), write each answer in the boxes running down.

Work out the sentences in any order you like; just be sure to match the number of the sentence with the number in the box. Put only one letter in each box. If all your answers are correct, all the words on the puzzle will fit together.

Clues Across

1. _____ the flour before you add it to the rest of the mixture.

2. She would often _____ on the other girls by hiding near where they were talking.

7. The giant Goliath laughed when he saw that his _____ was a boy armed only with a slingshot.

8. When she saw the gift in my hand, she made a _____ for where I was standing.

9. I bought a _____ of cheese at the dairy.

11. The men who offered to fix the roof for a thousand dollars were trying to _____ me of my money.

14. Water turns to ice if it is made cold enough and to _____ if it is made hot enough.

18. I heard the alarm clock _____, and I jumped out of bed.

19. The _____ was sometimes a simple tool, and other times a richly decorated ornament.

20. Don't _____ in and spoil their game of checkers by telling them how to move.

22. The _____ of Marie Curie shows her winning the Nobel Prize.

23. If the playing card has a shape like this ◊ on it, then it is called a _____.

24. The *Queen Mary* was a big, fast ship that could _____ across the Atlantic Ocean in five days.

Clues Down

1. The ocean was very calm, and there was almost no _____ at the beach.

2. The sheep looked very skinny after its _____ was clipped off.

3. Can you _____ the window open with this piece of folded newspaper?

4. I took a picture of her looking straight at the camera and another one in _____.

6. The last _____ of the campfire was just going out before we said goodnight and went to sleep.

10. He said he could _____ all seven of us into his small car.

12. The _____ was made of gold, and the front of it opened on two tiny hinges.

13. If a fire breaks out, we can _____ the building in five minutes.

15. She will _____ me in English and math every day after school.

16. Anyone trying to climb the castle walls could be pushed off into the _____.

17. A _____ is the hardest thing on earth and can be used to cut anything.

21. His hair turned from black to _____ and then to white.

WORD LIST 11

adult	bead	lecture
album	canal	suburb
author	comb	violet

adult—(noun) someone or something that is fully grown: *You must be an adult before you can vote.*—(adjective) **1.** fully grown; having reached full size: *The little kitten will become an adult cat.* **2.** suitable only for grown-up people: *Even though she is only ten, she loves to take part in adult conversations.*

album—(noun) **1.** a book with blank pages in which pictures or stamps can be kept: *I enjoy looking at the family photograph album.* **2.** a holder for a long-playing record; also the record itself: *I bought my grandmother an album of Greek folk music.*

author—(noun) a person who writes books, stories, or plays: *Beatrix Potter is the author of the Peter Rabbit stories.*

bead—(noun) **1.** a small, usually round, piece of wood, glass, or other material with a hole in it through which a string can be passed: *She has a pair of moccasins that are decorated with beads.* **2.** a small drop or bubble: *A bead of rain trickled down the window pane.*

canal—(noun) **1.** a waterway dug to allow ships and boats to cross through land: *The Suez Canal saves ships from having to sail all around Africa.* **2.** a ditch used to carry water for growing plants: *The canal brings water to the fields where there is little rain.*

comb—(noun) **1.** a thin strip of plastic or metal with many teeth. It is passed through the hair to smooth it down: *He said his hair was a mess because he couldn't find his comb.* **2.** the part that grows from the top of the head of hens, roosters, and some other kinds of birds: *A rooster's comb is bright red.*—(verb) **1.** to smooth down the hair with a comb: *Comb your hair before you leave.* **2.** to search all over with great care: *We must comb the house until we find the missing locket.*

lecture—(noun) a talk given to a class or audience: *The fire chief is giving a lecture on safety in the home.*—(verb) **1.** to give a talk before a class or audience: *She will lecture this afternoon on whales and dolphins.* **2.** to give a long scolding to: *No matter how much we lecture the girl, her manners do not improve.*

suburb—(noun) one of a number of towns that are close to, but separate from, a large city: *We live in a suburb of Chicago.*

violet—(noun) a small plant with flowers that are usually blue or purple: *The African violet is a popular house plant.*—(adjective) a color between blue and purple: *Do you think a violet blouse goes with a green skirt?*

EXERCISE 11A

Some of the sentences below are true and some are false. On the line to the left of each sentence, write *T* if you think the sentence is true, and *F* if you think the sentence is false.

_____ 1. Adult means fully grown.

_____ 2. An adult is a book, play, or movie for grown-ups.

_____ 3. An album is a book with blank pages in which pictures can be kept.

_____ 4. An album is a long-playing record.

_____ 5. An author is a talk given to a class or audience.

_____ 6. An author is a person who writes books.

_____ 7. A bead is the part that grows from the top of a rooster's head.

_____ 8. A bead is a small drop or bubble.

_____ 9. A canal is a waterway dug to allow ships to cross through land.

_____ 10. A canal is a ditch used to carry water for growing plants.

_____ 11. To comb the hair is to smooth it down.

_____ 12. To comb the town is to search all over it.

_____ 13. To lecture is to give a long scolding to.

_____ 14. To lecture is to give a talk to a class or audience.

_____ 15. A suburb is a large flat boat for carrying goods.

_____ 16. A suburb is a town that is close to, but separate from, a large city.

_____ 17. A violet is a small plant, usually with blue or purple flowers.

_____ 18. Violet is a color between blue and purple.

Check your answers against the correct ones below. They are not in order. This is to prevent your eye from catching sight of the correct answers before you have had a chance to do the exercise on your own.

4 T.	13 T.	7 F.	5 F.	15 F.	6 T.	2 F.	11 T.	17 T.
9 T.	12 T.	3 T.	10 T.	1 T.	8 T.	16 T.	14 T.	18 T.

EXERCISE 11B

Rewrite each sentence below. Replace the underlined words with the correct vocabulary word from Word List 11.

1. She wants to be a famous <u>writer of books and stories</u> when she is older.

   _____

   _____

2. The <u>fully-grown person</u> in charge of the children lets them play outside.

   _____

   _____

3. The <u>waterway dug to allow ships to cross through land</u> in Panama joins the Atlantic and Pacific Oceans.

   _____

   _____

4. He gave an interesting slide show and <u>talk before an audience</u> on Native American arts and crafts.

   _____

   _____

5. Each <u>small town lying near the big city</u> has its own local schools.

   _____

6. I lost a red <u>piece of glass with a hole through it</u> when I was making the bracelet.

   _____

   _____

7. A bird with a bright <u>part growing out of the top of its head </u>is able to spot easily another bird of the same kind.

   _____

   _____

8. The <u>book with blank pages in which stamps can be kept</u> has a cover that is <u>a color between blue and purple.</u>

   _____

   _____

EXERCISE 11C

In the boxes next to each definition, write the correct vocabulary word from Word List 11.
Put one letter in each box. If you do this properly, the long boxes running from top to bottom
will answer the following riddle:

Why is a good joke like the Liberty Bell?

1. a holder for a long-playing record; also the record itself

2. a small plant with flowers that are usually blue or purple

3. to give a talk to a class or audience

4. a person who writes books, stories, or plays

5. fully grown; having reached full size

6. a town that is close to, but not part of, a city

7. a color between blue and purple

8. to search all over with great care

9. a small drop or bubble

10. a ditch used to carry water for growing plants

11. a small, usually round, piece of glass, wood, or other material
    with a hole through which string can be passed

12. suitable only for grown-up people

55

WORD LIST 12

athlete   brand   tongs
autograph   disappear   vivid
balcony   evil

athlete—(noun) a person who takes part in sports: *An athlete has to train very hard for many years to become a world champion.*

autograph—(noun) something written in a person's own handwriting, especially that person's name: *I have the autograph of Michael Jordan, the famous basketball player.*—(verb) to write one's name on something: *The author will autograph his book for you.*

balcony—(noun) **1.** a part of a building that sticks out in the open air, usually with a low wall or railing around it: *Please step outside onto the balcony.* **2.** an upper level in a theater that sticks out over the main floor: *I got two front row seats in the balcony for the show.*

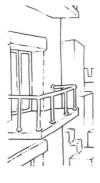

brand—(noun) **1.** a burning stick: *She snatched a brand from the fire.* **2.** a mark put on something to show who owns it: *The thieves changed the brand on the cows they stole.* **3.** a kind or make of something: *Which brand of butter do you prefer?*—(verb) **1.** to burn a mark upon: *The cowboys brand the cattle with hot irons.* **2.** to put a feeling of disgrace or shame upon: *They will brand her a coward for failing to save the children.*

disappear—(verb) **1.** to pass out of sight: *Watch the ship disappear in the mist on the lake.* **2.** to die out; to be no longer around: *How long ago did the dinosaurs disappear from the earth?*

evil—(noun) something that causes pain and suffering: *War is an evil.*—(adjective) being willing to do anything bad or wicked: *That evil person would rather hurt than help you.*

tongs—(noun) a tool that is used for gripping and holding things: *Use the tongs to pick up the hot embers.*

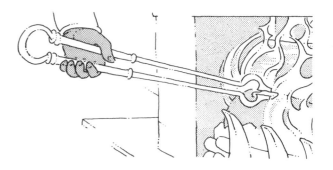

vivid—(adjective) **1.** very bright and strongly colored: *He wore a vivid shirt of red and orange.* **2.** giving a clear and strong picture in the mind: *The author's description of the fire was so vivid that I remember it well.*

EXERCISE 12A

Some of the sentences below are true and some are false. On the line to the left of each sentence, write _T_ if you think the sentence is true, and _F_ if you think the sentence is false.

_____ 1. An athlete is a part of a building that sticks out in the open air.

_____ 2. An athlete is a person who takes part in sports.

_____ 3. An autograph is a book with blank pages in which pictures can be kept.

_____ 4. An autograph is a person's name written in his or her own handwriting.

_____ 5. A balcony is an upper level in a theater that sticks out over the main floor.

_____ 6. A balcony is a part of a building that sticks out in the open air.

_____ 7. A brand is a burning stick.

_____ 8. A brand is a kind or make of something.

_____ 9. To brand a person is to put a feeling of disgrace upon him or her.

_____ 10. To brand an animal is to mark it with a hot iron.

_____ 11. To disappear is to go out of sight.

_____ 12. To disappear is to die out.

_____ 13. Evil means very bright and strongly colored.

_____ 14. Evil means being willing to do anything bad or wicked.

_____ 15. A pair of tongs is a tool used for cutting.

_____ 16. A pair of tongs is a tool used for gripping and holding things.

_____ 17. Vivid means giving a strong and clear picture in the mind.

_____ 18. Vivid means very bright and strongly colored.

Check your answers against the correct ones below. They are not in order. This is to prevent your eye from catching sight of the correct answers before you have had a chance to do the exercise on your own.

| 16 T. | 11 T. | 2 T. | 7 T. | 9 T. | 5 T. | 1 F. | 10 T. | 6 T. |
| 13 F. | 3 F. | 12 T. | 17 T. | 4 T. | 8 T. | 14 T. | 18 T. | 15 F. |

EXERCISE 12B

Rewrite each sentence below. Replace the underlined words with the correct vocabulary word from Word List 12.

1. He was so <u>willing to do wicked things</u> that everyone feared him.

   _____

   _____

2. He picked up the <u>burning stick</u> with the <u>tool for gripping and holding things.</u>

   _____

   _____

3. The <u>person who takes part in sports</u> said that when she was young she had polio and wore a brace on her leg in order to walk.

   _____

   _____

4. The witches in fairy tales are sometimes good, but sometimes they are <u>a cause of pain and suffering.</u>

   _____

   _____

5. The killing of millions of buffalo caused them almost to <u>be no longer around</u> in America.

   _____

   _____

6. We sat in the <u>upper level of the theater that sticks out over the main floor</u> to watch the play.

   _____

   _____

7. The memory of their first meeting was still <u>very clear in their minds</u> even after many years.

   _____

   _____

8. We watched the rabbits <u>pass out of sight</u> into the long grass.

   _____

   _____

EXERCISE 12C

In the boxes next to each definition, write the correct vocabulary word from Word List 12.
Put one letter in each box. If you do this properly, the long boxes running from top to bottom
will answer the following riddle:

Where is there always plenty of room?

1. a kind or make of something

2. a tool used for gripping and holding things

3. a part of a building that sticks out into the open air, usually with a low wall or fence around it

4. to write one's own name on something

5. a burning stick

6. very bright and strongly colored

7. to die out; to be no longer around

8. to put a feeling of disgrace or shame upon someone

9. an upper level in a theatre that sticks out above the main floor

10. giving a clear and strong picture in the mind

11. willing to do anything bad or wicked

12. something that causes great pain and suffering

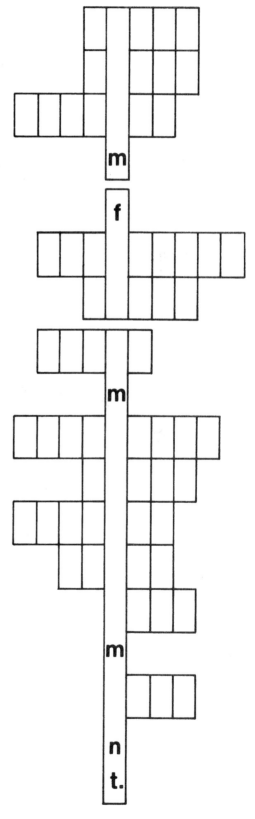

CROSSWORD 6

Decide what word from Word List 11 or 12 is missing from each sentence below. For the first group of sentences (Clues Across), write each answer in the boxes running across on the puzzle on the next page. For the second group (Clues Down), write each answer in the boxes running down.

Work out the sentences in any order you like; just be sure to match the number of the sentence with the number in the box. Put only one letter in each box. If all your answers are correct, all the words on the puzzle will fit together.

Clues Across

4. The dream I had was so _____ that I thought it was real.

5. A little _____ of sweat had formed on her nose.

6. Water travels from the lake to the fields along this _____.

9. The _____ is a pretty little flower that grows best in the shade.

10. _____ to pick up the lumps of sugar were placed on the table next to the bowl.

13. The _____ has five songs on one side and six on the other.

14. Chevy Chase is a _____ of Washington, D.C.

16. The highest prize for an _____ is an Olympic gold medal.

18. Hitler, who killed millions of people, must be one of the most _____ persons who ever lived.

20. His _____ had a few missing teeth, but he could still use it to arrange his hair.

22. The colors of the rainbow go from pink to _____.

23. People choose a _____ of soap they like and stay with it.

24. They will _____ her a traitor for having helped her country's foe.

Clues Down

1. Smoking cigarettes is an _____ that we cannot seem to stop.

2. Little Tony thinks it is an _____ book because it has no pictures.

3. Each apartment has its own _____ with a view of the river.

7. Mark Twain is the _____ of many books loved by people of all ages.

8. I asked the actress to _____ my program of the play.

11. An _____ pig is called a sow if it is female and a boar if it is male.

12. The children were hungry and soon made the cakes on the plate _____.

15. You get a fine view of the stage from the front row of the _____.

17. I shall _____ the boy for being late three days in a row.

19. You should wear _____ clothing when riding a bike at night.

21. I'll show you how to string the first _____ on the necklace, and then you can do the rest.